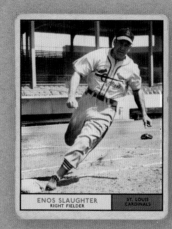

ENOS SLAUGHTER
RIGHT FIELDER

ST. LOUIS
CARDINALS

OZZIE SMITH
SHORTSTOP

ST. LOUIS
CARDINALS

THE STORY OF THE ST. LOUIS CARDINALS

Published by Creative Education
P.O. Box 227, Mankato, Minnesota 56002
Creative Education is an imprint of The Creative Company
www.thecreativecompany.us

Design and production by Blue Design
Art direction by Rita Marshall
Printed by Corporate Graphics in the United States of America

Photographs by Corbis (Bettmann), Getty Images (Bernstein Associates, Bruce Bennett Studios, Dan Donovan/MLB Photos, Elsa, FPG, Focus on Sport, Hulton Archive, G. Newman Lowrance, Brad Mangin/MLB Photos, MLB Photos, National Baseball Hall of Fame Library/MLB Photos, New York Times Company, Photo File, Louis Requena/MLB Photos, Josh Umphrey, Tim Umphrey, Ron Vesely/MLB Photos, Grey Villet/Time & Life Pictures, Dilip Vishwanat, Jeremy Woodhouse)

Library of Congress Cataloging-in-Publication Data

Gilbert, Sara.
The story of the St. Louis Cardinals / by Sara Gilbert.
p. cm. — (Baseball: the great American game)
Includes index.
Summary: The history of the St. Louis Cardinals professional baseball team from its inaugural 1882 season to today, spotlighting the team's greatest players and most memorable moments.
ISBN 978-1-60818-053-0
1. St. Louis Cardinals (Baseball team)—History—Juvenile literature. I. Title. II. Title: Saint Louis Cardinals. III. Series.

GV875.S74G45 2011
796.357'640977866—dc22   2010025217

CPSIA: 110310 PO1381

First Edition
9 8 7 6 5 4 3 2 1

Page 3: Pitcher Dizzy Dean
Page 4: Second baseman Skip Schumaker

BASEBALL: THE GREAT AMERICAN GAME

THE STORY OF THE ST. LOUIS CARDINALS

Sara Gilbert

CREATIVE EDUCATION

CONTENTS

COMING AND GOING

St. Louis, Missouri, became an official part of the United States when president Thomas Jefferson purchased Louisiana in 1803. A year later, it served as the starting point of the Lewis and Clark Expedition, which traveled west to the Pacific Ocean, mapping out the recently acquired territory along the way. Later, eager prospectors also departed from St. Louis, heading for California's mountains and dreaming of gold. Soon, St. Louis became the launching point for many westward travels, as families followed the Oregon and Santa Fe Trails in search of open land and new homes.

St. Louis's reputation as a place of transition carried over to its sports teams as well. The city's first professional ballclub, the Browns, joined baseball's eight-team National League (NL) in 1876 but lasted only two seasons. Professional baseball departed St. Louis until a new Browns team joined the American Association in 1882. That team signed a first baseman and manager named Charles Comiskey, who led the Browns to four straight pennants. Faced with a highly competitive baseball market, the American

St. Louis's 630-foot-tall Gateway Arch, built in the 1960s next to the Mississippi River, is one of the most famous monuments in the United States.

PITCHER · BOB GIBSON

Bob Gibson was a junkyard dog on the mound. "The meanest, nastiest pitcher I ever saw," said Cardinals catcher Tim McCarver. "There is no second place on this list." In fact, McCarver was reluctant to visit the mound during games because Gibson often became angry when he did. Batters were even less eager to face the intimidating hurler. Gibson threw high, tight heat and never apologized for hitting a batter. He made it a point not to make friends on opposing clubs; after pitching in each of his nine All-Star Games, he immediately left the ballpark to avoid sitting with other teams' players.

BOB GIBSON
PITCHER

STATS

Cardinals seasons: 1959–75

Height: 6-foot-1

Weight: 195

- **251–174 career record**

- **56 career shutouts**

- **2-time Cy Young Award winner**

- **Baseball Hall of Fame inductee (1981)**

Association and most of its teams folded in 1892, but four teams—including the Browns—were lucky enough to switch leagues and join the NL.

During the NL Browns' 7 straight losing seasons in St. Louis, the team changed managers 10 times. After a miserable 1898 season in which the Browns lost 111 games, the club was sold to Indiana businessmen Frank and Stanley Robinson, who also owned a team in Cleveland. Deeming St. Louis the better market, they gave their new team a boost by folding Cleveland's star players into the Browns' roster. Among those peddled players were hot-hitting outfielder Jesse Burkett and pitching ace Cy Young. The Robinsons also exchanged St. Louis's drab brown stockings for bright red ones, which prompted sportswriter Willie McHale to call the team the "Cardinals." The name stuck.

The new owners, the new name, and the new players made a tremendous difference for the Cardinals in 1899. Burkett hit .396, Young tallied a 26–16 record, and the Cardinals posted a much-improved record of 84–67 for the team's first winning season. But the positive impact of the changes didn't last long. Young defected to the new American League (AL) before the start of the 1901 season, and Burkett and other key players soon followed.

From 1904 to 1913, the Cardinals finished every season in the bottom half of the standings. Then, in 1914, St. Louis finished in third, riding the arm of spitball pitcher Bill Doak, who won 19 games that season. In 1915, second baseman Rogers "The Rajah" Hornsby played his first game for the Cardinals. By 1917, Hornsby was hitting well above .300 and helped the Cardinals reach a third-place finish with a record of 82–70. After years of trading leagues, players, managers, and owners, St. Louis seemed poised to find some steady success.

In Hornsby's 12 seasons with St. Louis, he would win 6 straight NL batting titles and eventually lead the team to its first World Series. Before that could happen, however, the Cardinals struggled to finish higher than third in the standings. Things changed in 1926, Hornsby's second season acting as player/manager. On the first day of spring training, he called a team meeting. "If there's anybody in this room who doesn't think we're going to win the pennant," he said, "go upstairs and get your money and go home, because we don't want you around here."

Rogers Hornsby was among the fastest players in baseball during his time, and he used his lively legs to record 30 career inside-the-park home runs.

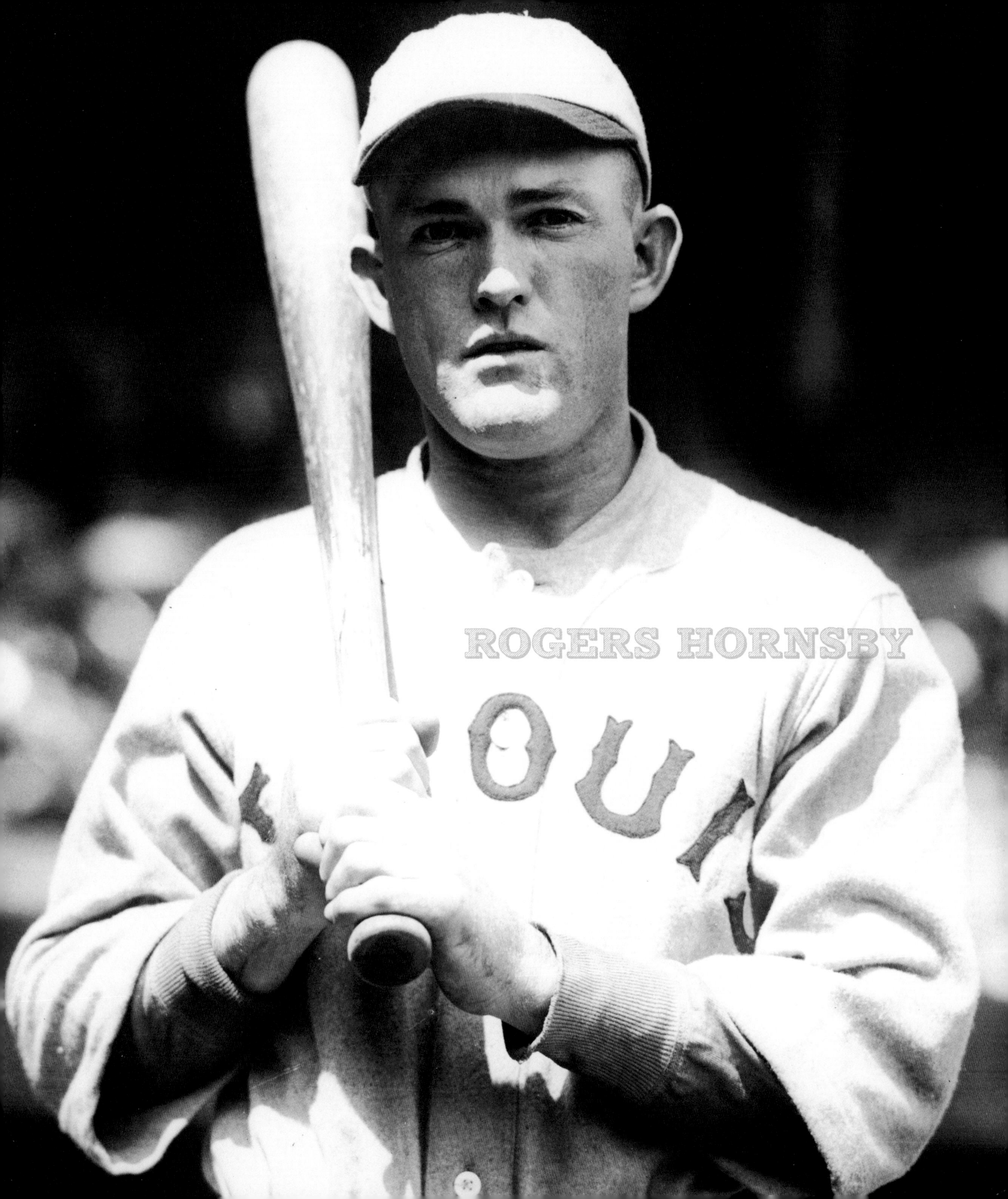
ROGERS HORNSBY

BRANCH RICKEY

FARMING BALLPLAYERS

In baseball's early years, like today, it was hard for many major-league teams to compete with wealthier clubs for the best ballplayers. In 1919, for example, the New York Giants offered St. Louis $300,000 for second baseman Rogers Hornsby as he was entering his prime. Cardinals general manager Branch Rickey turned the offer down, because he knew that selling off stars was no way to build a team. Good scouting wasn't enough, either—although the Cardinals' scouts were so well respected that other clubs would sometimes sign players the "Redbirds" showed interest in without ever having seen them play. Rickey believed in developing prospects, and he created a system that allowed him to do so. "I could find other Hornsbys," he said. "Pick them from the sandlots and keep them until they became stars. All I needed was a place to train them." So in 1919, the Cardinals started buying teams nationwide, eventually amassing more than 30 teams and 800 ballplayers. Players might take six years to reach the majors, but those who did were prepared. Every Cardinals star for 30 years, including outfielder Stan Musial, came through this farm system, now known as the minor leagues. And eventually, every big-league team copied the Cardinals' idea.

CATCHER · TED SIMMONS

Ted Simmons was not always a fan favorite, but that had no bearing on his play. A clutch switch hitter with power from both sides of the plate, he hit home runs batting both left- and right-handed in a single game three times. The fan friction came from Simmons's frustration with the team. During his 10 full Cardinals seasons, the team never made the postseason, and Simmons didn't hide his displeasure. "Winning," he once said. "That's all there is." A year after Simmons was traded in 1981, the Cardinals made it to the World Series. They faced—and defeated—his new team, the Milwaukee Brewers.

TED SIMMONS
CATCHER

ST. LOUIS
CARDINALS

STATS

Cardinals seasons: 1968–80

Height: 6 feet

Weight: 200

- .285 career BA

- 1,389 career RBI

- 8-time All-Star

- 2 pinch-hit grand slams

FIRST BASEMAN · ALBERT PUJOLS

Albert Pujols enjoyed one of the greatest professional starts in baseball history, reaching the majors after only one year in the minors and winning the 2001 NL Rookie of the Year award. His early batting numbers compared favorably with those of some of baseball's all-time greats—Ted Williams and Joe DiMaggio among them. Pujols's hitting prowess came from his smooth swing and hand speed. Showing patience and a keen eye rare in a slugger with his power, he scrutinized every pitch as long as possible before going "with the pitch," pulling inside pitches and knocking outside pitches to the opposite side of the field.

ALBERT PUJOLS
FIRST BASEMAN

STATS

Cardinals seasons: 2001–present

Height: 6-foot-3

Weight: 230

- 2003 NL leader in BA (.359)

- 3-time NL MVP

- 408 career HR

- 9-time All-Star

Of course, no one left. Together, the players helped their team claw its way up the standings. Flint Rhem, known for his blazing fastball, led the way on the mound, collecting 20 wins. And first baseman Jim Bottomley—known as "Sunny Jim" for his easygoing personality—contributed a league-leading 120 runs batted in (RBI). When the season ended, St. Louis had earned its first NL pennant. The Cardinals went on to win their first World Series, too, beating outfielder Babe Ruth and his New York Yankees four games to three.

WORLD SERIES AND WAR

Shockingly, St. Louis traded Hornsby away after the sensational 1926 season and brought in Frankie Frisch, a steady-hitting second baseman who led the Cardinals to the World Series in 1928, where they lost to the Yankees. Like Hornsby, Frisch eventually managed the team. The feisty Frisch was famous for jawing at umpires, once sauntering onto a wet field under an umbrella to argue that the game should be called due to rain. (He was ejected, and the game continued.)

St. Louis continued winning into the next decade as well. In 1930, the Cardinals took the NL pennant and met the Philadelphia Athletics in the World Series, losing in six games. The same two teams clashed in the 1931 World Series, where center fielder Johnny "Pepper" Martin was the star, despite Frisch being honored as the NL Most Valuable Player (MVP). Martin led the Redbirds to victory with 12 hits in 24 at bats, including a home run and 4 doubles. He knocked in five runs and scored five more himself, stealing five bases along the way. "So I did all right," the humble Martin said later, "but I sure never looked for no series hero role, and, anyway, my stealing five bases wasn't because I wanted to show off or anything."

In 1932, pitcher Dizzy Dean and outfielder Joe "Ducky" Medwick joined the team. Dean threw all strikes, ringing up 191 batters in 1932 with his overpowering fastball and curve, and Medwick later captured the Triple Crown (leading the league in batting average, home runs, and RBI) in 1937.

Dean and Medwick, along with Frisch and Martin, formed the heart of the "Gashouse Gang," a Cardinals squad known for its wild play and off-field antics. But the Gashouse Gang's talent was no joke. In 1934, they

CARDINALS

PEPPER MARTIN

Pepper Martin, nicknamed "The Wild Horse of the Osage," led the league in steals in 1933, 1934, and 1936. His aggressive running made him a valuable member of the Gashouse Gang and a four-time All-Star.

SECOND BASEMAN · ROGERS HORNSBY

Rogers Hornsby didn't read books or watch movies because he feared it would hurt his eyes. And it may have paid off. One of the best hitters of all time (with a lifetime batting average of .358, second only to Detroit Tigers outfielder Ty Cobb), Hornsby's gray eyes knew the strike zone and were described by one reporter as a "gunfighter's calculating eyes." A story goes that when one young opposing pitcher complained about the lack of called strikes during a Hornsby at bat, the umpire replied, "Son, when you throw a strike, Mr. Hornsby will let you know."

ROGERS HORNSBY
SECOND BASEMAN

STATS

Cardinals seasons: 1915–26, 1933

Height: 5-foot-11

Weight: 175

- 2-time NL Triple Crown winner

- 1,584 career RBI

- Career-high .424 BA (1924)

- Baseball Hall of Fame inductee (1942)

won the NL pennant with a 95–58 record. That season, Dean and his brother, pitcher Paul "Daffy" Dean, were unhittable. Dizzy won 30 games, and Daffy notched 19. Before the World Series against the Detroit Tigers, Dizzy predicted that he and Daffy would win two games apiece—and they did, giving St. Louis another world championship.

The team won 96 games the following year but not the pennant. In 1937, Dizzy Dean broke a toe when he was hit by a line drive. He returned to the mound before it healed, causing further damage, and never regained his dominant form. The Gang, it seemed, had run out of gas.

St. Louis struggled until 1941—the year that America entered World War II—when it finished behind only the Brooklyn Dodgers in the standings. In 1942, the Cardinals won 42 of their last 52 games and stole the NL pennant from Brooklyn. Besides smooth-fielding shortstop Marty Marion, the team included pitchers Johnny Beazley and Mort Cooper (who won the NL MVP award that year) and outfielders Enos "Country" Slaughter and Stan "The Man" Musial, who was known for his personable nature and marvelous hitting. The Cardinals met the

ENOS SLAUGHTER

heavily favored Yankees in the 1942 World Series. St. Louis was nearly no-hit in Game 1 but rallied for four runs in the eighth inning. The team lost that game but gained the momentum, winning the next four games for the championship.

By 1943, many ballplayers had left baseball to fight in the war; the Cardinals lost both Beazley and Slaughter to the armed forces. But although some teams were thoroughly depleted, St. Louis remained strong, since some of its key players had been exempted from the military draft for health reasons.

Musial put together his first legendary season in 1943 and won his first NL MVP award after leading the league in batting at .357. He and Cooper took St. Louis to a second straight World Series showdown with the Yankees. This time, St. Louis was heavily favored, but the Yankees prevailed, four games to one. St. Louis won its third straight pennant in 1944, and Marion became the third Cardinals player in a row to be named league MVP. The Redbirds faced the AL's St. Louis Browns in the World Series and beat their hometown rivals to earn top-dog standing in Missouri's largest city.

AN UNLIKELY HERO

Late in the 1926 season, St. Louis signed pitcher Grover Cleveland Alexander. Although he was one of the winningest hurlers in baseball history, Alexander had his problems. He was haunted by his combat experiences in World War I and battled both alcoholism and epilepsy. At 39 years old, he continued to play because baseball was all he had—and because he was still quite good at it. His fastball rode in on right-handed hitters, and his curveball broke sharply away. The Cardinals hoped he would give them a boost—and he delivered, winning nine games in the last two months of the season. But it was Alexander's contributions during the 1926 World Series that earned him a special place in Cardinals lore. After the Redbirds lost Game 1 to a New York Yankees lineup that included Babe Ruth and Lou Gehrig, Alexander controlled the Yankees for a nine-inning Game 2 victory and did the same in Game 6. One night later, with the bases loaded in the seventh, Alexander came on and struck out slugging Yankees second baseman Tony Lazzeri to preserve a 3–2 lead. He then pitched two shutout innings to ensure the Cardinals' victory, concluding a heroic performance by an unlikely hero.

SPARKS FLY IN ST. LOUIS

n 1945, Musial and several other players were finally called to military service, and the Cardinals fell three games short of a fourth straight pennant. But when he and all of baseball's stars returned from war for the 1946 season, the Cardinals came together as if no time had passed. Two newcomers, pitcher Howie Pollett and second baseman Albert "Red" Schoendienst, made strong contributions during a tight pennant race that ended with St. Louis and Brooklyn tied 98–58. St. Louis won a special three-game playoff and went on to beat the Boston Red Sox in a seven-game World Series.

The run of four pennants in five years ended after 1946, but the Cardinals continued to contend, finishing second in 1947, 1948, and 1949. However, a new decade did not bring more championships to St. Louis's Busch Stadium. Musial still played like a star throughout the 1950s, collecting his 3,000th hit in 1958, and such talented players as third baseman Ken Boyer, pitcher Bob Gibson, and catcher Tim McCarver played well for the Cardinals. But a second-place finish in 1957 was the closest the team could come to a pennant.

THIRD BASEMAN · KEN BOYER

Ken Boyer, the Cardinals' soft-spoken captain, led by example, making noise with big plays rather than big words. A terrific all-around player, he swung a consistently powerful bat and wielded a sticky glove at the "hot corner." It was no coincidence that Boyer's 1964 MVP season was the same year that St. Louis returned to the World Series after an 18-year absence. In that World Series, he led his team to victory over the New York Yankees, scoring five runs and knocking in six more in a startling four-games-to-three win that netted the Cards their eighth world championship.

KEN BOYER
THIRD BASEMAN

ST. LOUIS
CARDINALS

STATS

Cardinals seasons: 1955–65 (as player), 1978–80 (as manager)

Height: 6-foot-2

Weight: 200

• Twice hit for the cycle (a single, double, triple, and HR in the same game)

• 5-time Gold Glove winner

• 7-time All-Star

• 1964 NL MVP

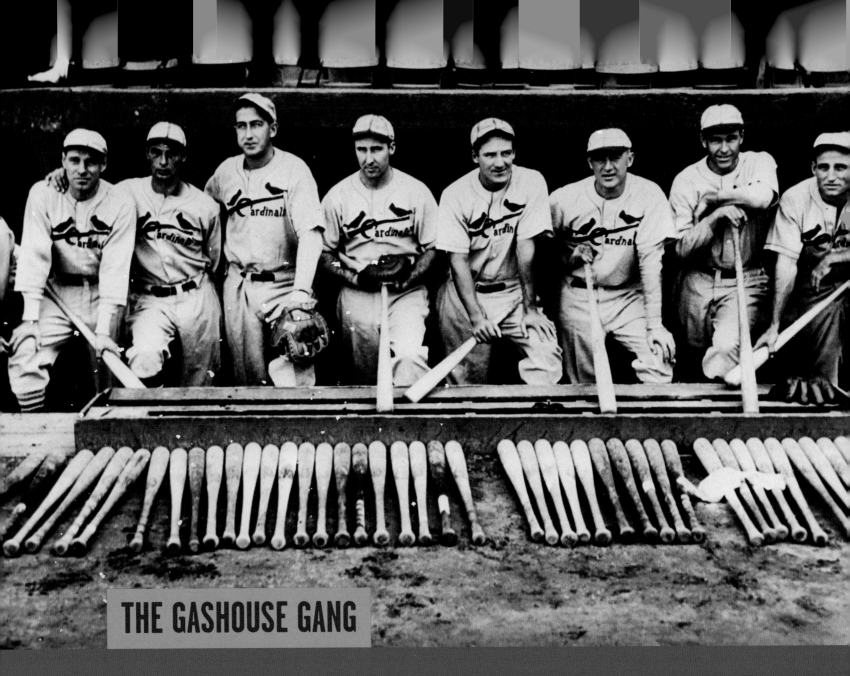

THE GASHOUSE GANG

The Cardinals of the mid-1930s were known as the "Gashouse Gang," a rowdy crew both on and off the field. Pitcher Dizzy Dean, center fielder Pepper Martin, left fielder Ducky Medwick, first baseman Ripper Collins, shortstop Leo Durocher, and second baseman and manager Frankie Frisch combined to create an explosive mix of personalities. Dean, Martin, Collins, and Durocher were jokesters, while the irritable Medwick and excitable Frisch were often on the receiving end of the ribbing. Once, Martin took aim at Frisch with a water balloon from a fifth-floor hotel window. And Martin would often give an unsuspecting teammate on the bench a "hot foot," sticking a lit match in his shoe. Dean, meanwhile, liked to hand out exploding cigars. But the hooliganism wasn't all aimed at teammates. Members of the Gang were known to throw sneezing powder into hotel ceiling fans or burst in on banquets, pretending to be workmen. One story goes that during a blazing summer day, Gang members in fur coats built a campfire in front of the dugout. Luckily for Cardinals fans, the Gang played baseball with the same energy and joy they put into their antics, which helped them win the 1934 World Series.

Lou Brock's base-stealing heroics are today commemorated in the Lou Brock Award, given each season to the NL's top base stealer.

It wasn't until 1964 that St. Louis would regain its lofty status. That year, a speedy castoff from the Chicago Cubs joined the team—left fielder Lou Brock. Brock's arrival jumpstarted the team. He was a spark plug whose hitting and, especially, base running made good things happen. His speed, combined with Boyer's hustle and Gibson's high, tight fastballs, brought another NL pennant to St. Louis.

When St. Louis faced the Yankees in the 1964 World Series, Boyer played against his brother, Clete, New York's third baseman. The two brothers gave the term "sibling rivalry" new meaning in the series. Ken knocked in the series' first run, but Clete singled, stole second base, and scored in the next inning. In Games 2 and 3, Clete knocked in runs to help New York win, and it seemed he and the Yankees might get the better of Ken and the Cardinals. But in a pivotal Game 4, Ken bashed a grand slam for a 4–3 Cardinals victory. Each Boyer brother banged a round-tripper in Game 7, but it was Ken's that helped the winning cause, as St. Louis earned its seventh World Series title. Still, the series was a thriller for both sides. "That week was the most fun I ever had," Clete said.

Like all great Cardinals teams, this one was not satisfied with a single championship. The 1967 Cardinals met the Red Sox in another World Series that went seven games and ended in a Cardinals victory. Slugging Cardinals first baseman Orlando Cepeda garnered NL MVP honors that season, while McCarver was runner-up for the award. However, Brock and Gibson led the team when it counted most.

Gibson proved that he wasn't just tough to hit—he was tough in every sense of the word. He returned from two months on the disabled list to pitch three complete games in the World Series, allowing only three total runs. "Invincible," McCarver later said of Gibson's performance. "He just dominated the series." Brock, meanwhile, had kept things moving on offense with 12 hits, 7 stolen bases, and 8 runs throughout the series. The next year, McCarver and Brock again led the Cardinals to the NL pennant, but this time, St. Louis lost the "Fall Classic" to Detroit.

The 1967 World Series was a tight battle that saw the Cardinals and Red Sox
each win a road game. The Cardinals ran away to victory in Game 7, thanks
largely to a three-run homer by second baseman Julian Javier (pictured).

SHORTSTOP · OZZIE SMITH

Ozzie Smith did a backflip when he took the field for each home game—and that was only the beginning. Nicknamed "The Wizard of Oz" because of his seemingly magical glove, Smith was known for gravity-defying feats. He could dive, pop up, and then throw as if such plays were routine. Whereas another infielder might knock down a hard-hit ground ball, The Wizard would snag it cleanly and gun down the runner. His manager, Whitey Herzog, claimed that Smith's defense saved 75 runs a year. Smith worked hard at offense, too, progressing throughout his career from being an easy out to an offensive threat.

OZZIE SMITH
SHORTSTOP

STATS

Cardinals seasons: 1982–96

Height: 5-foot-11

Weight: 150

- 13-time Gold Glove winner

- Only 8 fielding errors in 1991

- Career-high .303 BA (1987)

- Baseball Hall of Fame inductee (2002)

Although Gibson and Brock were with the Cardinals throughout the 1970s, as were stars such as third baseman Joe Torre and catcher Ted Simmons, the team finished no higher than second place in the newly formed NL Eastern Division. Throughout most of the decade, the team lacked either pitching or power—or both.

FLIPS AND FAST FEET

T he Cardinals found ways to win during the 1980s with almost no power at all but with the help of manager Whitey Herzog. In 1982, the team hit only 67 homers but managed to collect 685 runs, most of which were gained just 1 base at a time. St. Louis won with speed and defense instead. Outfielder Lonnie Smith led the charge around the base paths with 68 stolen bases, while acrobatic shortstop Ozzie "The Wizard of Oz" Smith kept opposing players off the bases with his magical glove work—and kept fans entertained with the backflips he did as he took the field for each home game. First baseman Keith Hernandez, center fielder Willie McGee, and

LEFT FIELDER · STAN MUSIAL

Stan Musial was the complete ballplayer. In 1948, when he won his third NL MVP award, he led the league in batting average, hits, doubles, triples, runs, RBI, total bases, and slugging percentage. He was one blast shy of the home run lead that season as well. He scored and knocked in an average of 104 runs each year during his 21 complete seasons. Other teams knew they were in the presence of greatness when they played the Cards. It was in Brooklyn that Musial became known as "Stan the Man," because Dodgers fans bemoaned each of his plate appearances by saying, "Here comes the man."

STAN MUSIAL
LEFT FIELDER

STATS

Cardinals seasons: 1941–63

Height: 6 feet

Weight: 175

- 3,630 career hits

- 20-time All-Star

- 9 career grand slams

- Baseball Hall of Fame inductee (1969)

SPORTSMAN'S PARK

SHARING ST. LOUIS

Once upon a time, two Browns baseball teams shared St. Louis: the NL Browns, who became the St. Louis Cardinals, and the AL Browns, who in 1954 became the Baltimore Orioles. Those two teams shared Sportsman's Park for 34 years. And in 1944, they shared the World Series spotlight. What the two teams did not have in common was a winning tradition. For the Cardinals, 1944 was their third World Series in a row. For the Browns, it was their first and only appearance. But the Browns did share one more thing with the Cardinals—the fans. Most people just didn't see the teams as being in competition with each other. The 1944 series was called the "Trolley Series," named for the most popular way of getting to the park. But once the fans arrived, they didn't quite know how to react as the Cardinals won the series in six games. "It was the quietest World Series ever," said Luke Sewell, manager of the AL Browns. "I don't think the fans knew who to root for. They'd been waiting all their lives for this, and when it finally came to be, they just sat and took it all in without too much cheering."

CARDINALS

BRUCE SUTTER

closer Bruce Sutter also used their gloves and arms to help limit opponents to an NL-low 609 runs.

By season's end, the Cardinals were NL East champs. After topping the Atlanta Braves in three games in the NL Championship Series (NLCS), the Redbirds were back in the Fall Classic. In the World Series, the light-hitting Cardinals faced a bruising Milwaukee Brewers lineup that had led the AL in home runs and runs scored. But it was the Cardinals who outscored the Brewers, averaging an uncharacteristic five runs per game.

Hernandez scored four runs and knocked in eight himself, while staff ace Joaquin Andujar—known for his ornery mood on the days he pitched—won two games with his shifting fastball and slider. Sutter also collected a win and two saves as the Cardinals took the series four games to three. "There were a lot of people around baseball—writers mostly—who just couldn't believe the Cardinals were world champions," Herzog said. "They seemed to think there was something wrong

Bruce Sutter spent four seasons in St. Louis, using his deadly split-finger fastball to forge a reputation as one of the game's all-time great closers.

with the way we played baseball, with speed and defense and line-drive hitters."

Just three years later, the Cardinals found themselves back in the World Series. Although the team's philosophy was the same—run fast and play great defense—its lineup had changed. Left fielder Vince Coleman, who stole an incredible 110 bases and won NL Rookie of the Year honors, now manned the outfield with McGee, and pitcher John Tudor combined with Andujar for 42 victories. But the retooled Cardinals could not capture their 10th World Series trophy, losing to a fellow Missouri franchise, the Kansas City Royals, 4 games to 3.

In 1987, the Cardinals claimed their third pennant of the decade but again lost the World Series in seven games. This time they battled the Minnesota Twins, who proved unstoppable in Minneapolis's Metrodome, winning all four games there. St. Louis would have to wait nearly 10 years before reaching the postseason again.

The early 1990s were tough years for Cardinals fans accustomed to greatness. The best the Redbirds could manage from 1990 to 1995 was second place in the NL East, then the NL Central (to which St. Louis was

CENTER FIELDER · WILLIE McGEE

Willie McGee was a gift from the New York Yankees. In 1981, with too many outfielders and not enough pitchers, the Yankees traded McGee to St. Louis for relief pitcher Bob Sykes. McGee turned into the Cardinals' best center fielder ever—a line-drive-hitting speedster with a sure glove. He led St. Louis to three NL pennants and one world championship during his tenure with the team. In Game 3 of the 1982 World Series, he made a leaping catch to rob Milwaukee Brewers slugger Gorman Thomas of a home run and hit two homers of his own in the Cardinals victory.

WILLIE McGEE
CENTER FIELDER

ST. LOUIS CARDINALS

STATS

Cardinals seasons: 1982–90, 1996–99

Height: 6-foot-1

Weight: 175

- **3-time Gold Glove winner**

- **1985 NL MVP**

- **2-time NL leader in BA**

- **.295 career BA**

MARK McGWIRE

reassigned in 1994). But in 1996, under new manager Tony La Russa, St. Louis finally ended its postseason drought. Led by outfielders Ray Lankford and Brian Jordan, the Redbirds climbed from nine games under .500 in May to win the NL Central with an 88–74 record. They swept the San Diego Padres in a first-round playoff series but lost to the Atlanta Braves in a seven-game NLCS.

Despite a steady barrage of home runs by powerful first baseman Mark McGwire, St. Louis could not find its way above third place for the rest of the '90s. But as the decade ended, Cardinals fans had reason to believe that the team was ready to return to its winning ways.

WINNING AGAIN

t. Louis made the playoffs six times in the seven seasons from 2000 through 2005. Center fielder Jim Edmonds led the resurgence with steady hitting and spectacular over-the-shoulder catches, while sweet-swinging first baseman Albert Pujols took the league by storm with 130 RBI during his 2001 rookie season. On the mound, pitchers such as Matt Morris and Chris Carpenter piled up wins, while closer Jason Isringhausen slammed the door on opposing offenses.

In its first three playoff trips in the new millennium, St. Louis fell short of the World Series. But in 2004, the Cardinals rebounded from a slow start in the spring to capture first place in the NL Central by mid-June—a spot the team refused to relinquish for the rest of the season. With an amazing 105–57 record, the Cardinals won the division, then beat the Los Angeles Dodgers in the NL Division Series (NLDS) and the Houston Astros in a seven-game NLCS. The Redbirds could not capture that elusive 10th title,

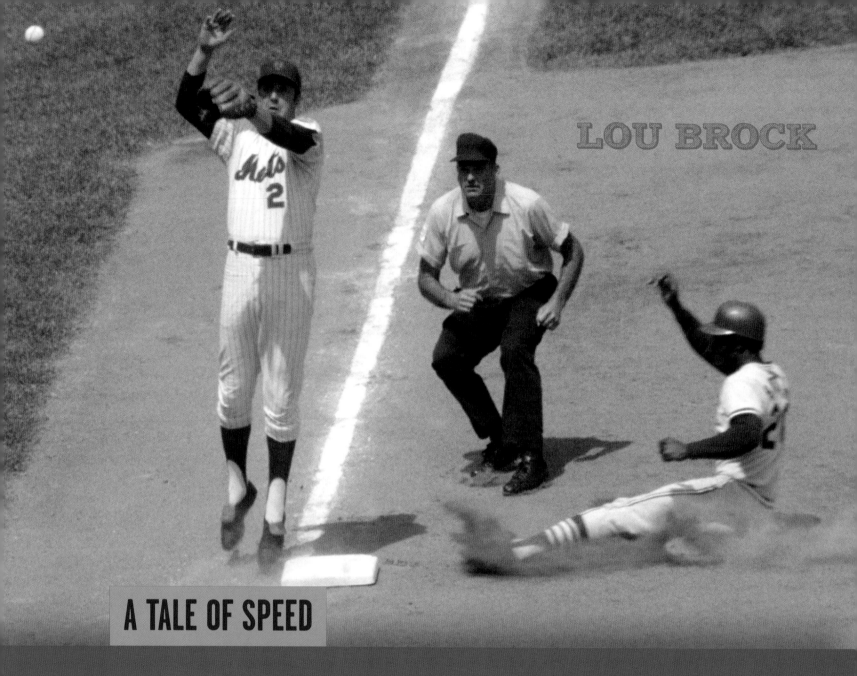

LOU BROCK

A TALE OF SPEED

Left fielder Lou Brock was all about speed. In 1961, he got off to a blazing start with Minnesota's minor-league St. Cloud Rox. He hit .361, scored 117 runs, and was quickly promoted to the Chicago Cubs' roster that same year. But during his four years in Chicago, Brock's career slowed and nearly stalled as he struggled mightily at the plate. When he was traded to St. Louis in 1964, the move was not popular with Cardinals fans or teammates. But manager Johnny Keane saw something in Brock. "To play regularly on this club," he told Brock, "you have to steal bases.

You go anytime, go anywhere, and if anybody asks you about it, you tell them where to go." And so Brock went. That season, he stole 33 bases for St. Louis, which ignited his hitting and his career. Brock went on to break Los Angeles Dodgers shortstop Maury Wills's single-season stolen base record of 104 with 118 thefts in 1974. And 3 years later, he broke Detroit Tigers outfielder Ty Cobb's lifetime stolen base mark of 893, finishing his career with 938 pilfered bags. Brock's lively legs carried him right into the Hall of Fame, which he entered in 1985.

CARDINALS

RIGHT FIELDER · ENOS SLAUGHTER

Enos "Country" Slaughter hustled—every play, every hit, every out. But he didn't start out that way. As a young man in the Cardinals' minor-league system, Slaughter played under manager Eddie Dyer. During one particularly bad game, the sulky outfielder walked slowly to the dugout between innings. "Son," Dyer said, "if you're tired, we'll try to get you some help."

Slaughter caught Dyer's meaning. He wasn't about to lose playing time because of a poor attitude or a lack of hustle. "That's when I started running," he said. Slaughter eventually ran all the way into the Hall of Fame.

STATS

Cardinals seasons: 1938–53

Height: 5-foot-9

Weight: 185

- .300 career BA

- 10-time All-Star

- 1942 NL leader in hits (188)

- Baseball Hall of Fame inductee (1985)

ENOS SLAUGHTER
RIGHT FIELDER

ST. LOUIS CARDINALS

CARDINALS

MANAGER · WHITEY HERZOG

Whitey Herzog had his own style of baseball. "Whitey Ball," it was called, and it was meant to be played on an artificial grass surface known as AstroTurf. Herzog honed this strategy—built on speed and defense—with the Kansas City Royals. He managed there for five years, winning the AL Western Division three times but never advancing further.

When the Royals fired him after the 1979 season, Herzog joined the Cardinals, whose stadium also featured AstroTurf. He implemented the same strategy—with even better results. His Cardinals teams reached the World Series three times, winning it in 1982.

STATS

Cardinals seasons as manager: 1980–90

Managerial record: 1,281–1,125

World Series championship: 1982

WHITEY HERZOG
MANAGER

though, losing in four straight games to the red-hot Boston Red Sox in the World Series. They maintained their hold on first place in the division the next season as well, again returning to the NLCS, where they were turned away by the Astros.

The Cardinals' 83–78 record in 2006 allowed them to just barely make the playoffs. However, then they went on a tear. After beating the San Diego Padres in the NLDS and the New York Mets in the NLCS, the Cardinals stomped the Tigers four games to one to win the World Series. As fireworks exploded in the sky above St. Louis's Busch Stadium, the Cardinals ran onto the field to celebrate their 10th world championship. "I think we shocked the world," said Edmonds.

St. Louis fans didn't want to miss any surprises the following season. But many of the club-record 3,552,180 fans who came out to watch the team's home games in 2007 left the stadium disappointed. Despite solid play by Pujols, Edmonds, and catcher Yadier Molina, the

JIM EDMONDS

RYAN FRANKLIN

Cardinals fell below the .500 mark for the first time since 1999. Despite rallying to a winning record the following season, the Cards again stayed home during the playoffs in 2008.

That disappointing trend changed in 2009, when the Cardinals rose above predictions of a subpar season to win the NL Central with a 91–71 record. Pujols claimed his third MVP award, and Ryan Franklin emerged as the team's new closer. But it may have been two midseason trades that truly made the difference for the 2009 Cardinals. In the span of two days, St. Louis traded for slugging left fielder Matt Holliday and

JACK BUCK

LOSING THEIR VOICE

When Bob Gibson pitched a no-hitter in 1971, it was Jack Buck who described the pitcher mopping his brow, getting the sign, and throwing a called strike for the final out. When Lou Brock stole his 105th base in 1974, it was Buck who let Cardinals fans know that the speedster had set an almost unfathomable record. When Mark McGwire tied Roger Maris's single-season record with home run number 61 in 1998, it was Buck who yelled, "Looky there! Looky there! Number 61!" and who then asked for a moment so he could join the cheering fans. "Pardon me while I stand up and applaud," he said. Buck's gravelly voice called all the Cardinals' most memorable moments for nearly 50 years. The legendary broadcaster first sat behind the microphone at Busch Stadium in 1954 and stayed there until health problems led to his retirement in 2001. By then, Buck, who also called football and baseball games for the CBS network, had announced 11 World Series, 18 Super Bowls, and 4 All-Star Games. Buck's death at the age of 77 in 2002 saddened the St. Louis community. More than 10,000 fans attended his memorial service at Busch Stadium.

CARDINALS

ALBERT PUJOLS

In 2010, Albert Pujols posted his 10th consecutive season with at least 30 home runs and 100 RBI—a feat no other player had ever accomplished.

COLBY RASMUS

hard-hitting second baseman Julio Lugo. The team's revamped offense quickly got hot, winning 20 games in August. But those bats went cold in the playoffs, and the Dodgers swept St. Louis in a three-game NLDS. Unfortunately, in 2010, not even a 20-win season by ace pitcher Adam Wainwright could get the Cards to the playoffs.

If history is any guide, St. Louis fans can look forward to stronger seasons ahead. Already, the Cardinals are one of the most decorated franchises in all of baseball, with 10 World Series trophies proudly displayed at Busch Stadium, and more than 15 players enshrined in the Hall of Fame. It should be no surprise that the Redbirds are planning to fly away with another world championship soon.

MATT HOLLIDAY

INDEX